100 QUESTIONS about COLONIAL AMERICA

and all the answers too!

Written and Illustrated by
Simon Abbott

PETER PAUPER PRESS, INC.
White Plains, New York

PETER PAUPER PRESS

In 1928, at the age of twenty-two, Peter Beilenson began printing books on a small press in the basement of his parents' home in Larchmont, New York. Peter—and later, his wife, Edna—sought to create fine books that sold at "prices even a pauper could afford."

Today, still family owned and operated, Peter Pauper Press continues to honor our founders' legacy of quality, value, and fun for big kids and small kids alike.

Designed by Heather Zschock

Text and illustrations copyright © 2018 by Simon Abbott

Published by Peter Pauper Press, Inc.
202 Mamaroneck Avenue
White Plains, New York 10601 USA

Published in the United Kingdom and Europe by Peter Pauper Press, Inc.
c/o White Pebble International
Unit 2, Plot 11 Terminus Rd.
Chichester, West Sussex PO19 8TX, UK

Library of Congress Cataloging-in-Publication Data
Names: Abbott, Simon, 1967- author, illustrator.
Title: 100 questions about colonial America : and all the answers too! /
written and illustrated by Simon Abbott.
Other titles: One hundred questions about colonial America
Description: White Plains, New York : Peter Pauper Press, 2018.
Identifiers: LCCN 2017053106 | ISBN 9781441326164 (hardcover : alk. paper)
Subjects: LCSH: United States--History--Colonial period, ca.
1600-1775--Juvenile literature. | United States--Social life and
customs--To 1775--Juvenile literature. | Questions and answers.
Classification: LCC E188 .A24 2018 | DDC 973.2--dc23 LC record available at https://lccn.loc.
gov/2017053106
ISBN 978-1-4413-2616-4
Manufactured for Peter Pauper Press, Inc.
Printed in Hong Kong

7 6 5 4 3 2 1

Visit us at www.peterpauper.com

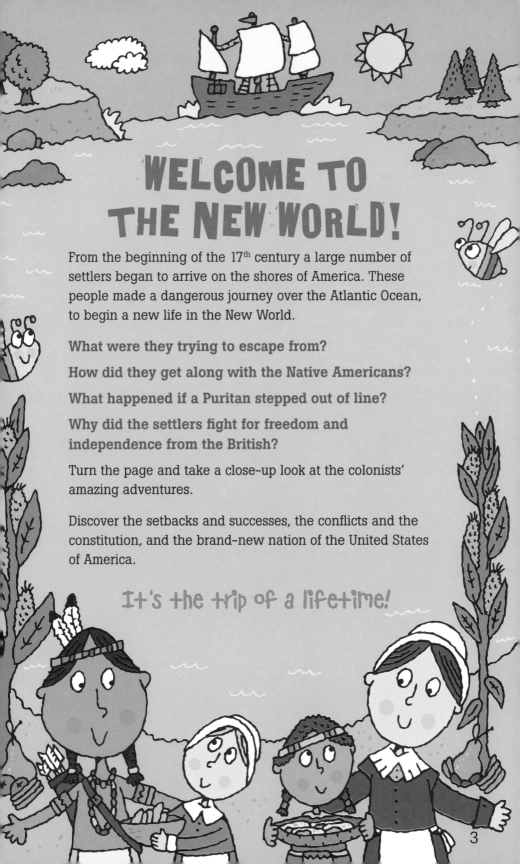

WELCOME TO THE NEW WORLD!

From the beginning of the 17th century a large number of settlers began to arrive on the shores of America. These people made a dangerous journey over the Atlantic Ocean, to begin a new life in the New World.

What were they trying to escape from?

How did they get along with the Native Americans?

What happened if a Puritan stepped out of line?

Why did the settlers fight for freedom and independence from the British?

Turn the page and take a close-up look at the colonists' amazing adventures.

Discover the setbacks and successes, the conflicts and the constitution, and the brand-new nation of the United States of America.

It's the trip of a lifetime!

3

SETTING THE SCENE

A long time ago, the United States looked very different. For one thing, it didn't have states! Let's take a look at the Europeans who sailed across the Atlantic to build new lives, and how they formed the first thirteen colonies.

When did colonial life in America begin?
Good question! Although outposts had been founded by the English and Spanish adventurers in the late 1500s, our story begins with the Jamestown settlement in 1607.

How long is the colonial period?
The colonial period stretches nearly 170 years, from the first settlement to the Declaration of Independence in 1776. During this time, the colonies grew from a hodgepodge of settlements into a united country, rising up against British control, and demanding their freedom.

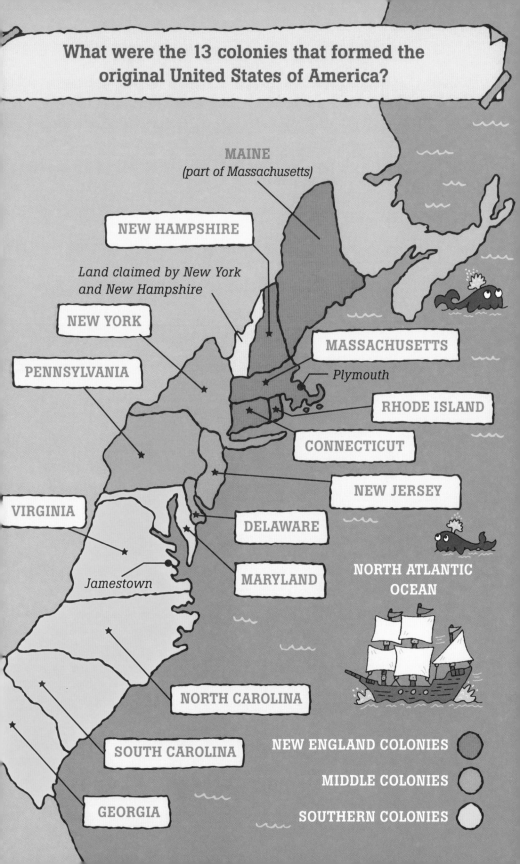

TAKE A LOOK AT THE SETTLERS' TIMELINE

This handy fact sheet gives you all the key dates you need, as you begin your discovery of Colonial America.

1565: The first Spanish colony in Florida

1585: The Roanoke Colony founded by Sir Walter Raleigh

1607: First permanent settlement in the New World— Jamestown, Virginia

1620: The Pilgrims land at Plymouth Rock, Massachusetts.

1621: The First Thanksgiving

1623: New Hampshire is founded.

1629: The Great Migration of European settlers to the New World begins.

1630: Boston is founded by the Puritans.

1634: Maryland is founded.

1636: Rhode Island is founded by Roger Williams.

1664: New York and New Jersey are founded.

1681: The founding of Pennsylvania by William Penn

1732: Georgia is founded by James Oglethorpe.

1756: The French and Indian War begins.

1765: The Stamp Act

1770: Boston Massacre occurs.

1773: The Boston Tea Party

1774: The first Continental Congress

1775: Beginning of the Revolutionary War

1776: The Declaration of Independence

1783: The Treaty of Paris and the end of the Revolutionary War

1789: George Washington becomes the first President of the United States.

ANCHORS AWEIGH!

Whether it was to explore a new world or to find the freedom to create their own community, people took the trip across the ocean for many different reasons. Let's find out why!

Why did explorers set their sights on America?
There were many reasons, but we can break them down into four main categories:

1. Money
2. Religion
3. Politics
4. Social

Let's begin with money!
Why did they think they could get rich in the new land?
A new continent meant plenty of space on which cash crops (crops that farmers sell instead of using themselves) like sugar, cotton, and tobacco could be grown in large quantities. It was also an ocean away from the hardships of the Old World, where prices for day-to-day items like bread or a roof over one's head were so high they forced some people into poverty and debt.

What sort of support did these explorers have?
They got an OK from the top of the pile! Kings and queens looked to America as a way of expanding their empires, and granted charters to enterprising businesses to search for gold and silver and other resources.

Don't forget your passport!

Why would religion be one reason that the settlers would go to the New World?
In some of their home countries, there were laws that kept people from practicing their own religion. So groups like the Puritans (or Pilgrims), Quakers, Catholics, and the Jewish people all saw the wide-open spaces of the New World as places where they could form their own communities and practice in peace.

Finally, what about the social and political reasons?

There was a social divide between the wealthy and the poor in the Old World, and if you were poor, you often stayed poor. The New World put everyone on an equal footing at first, so it meant anyone could have an opportunity to get ahead, not just the rich.

What if you didn't have enough money to pay for a boat ticket to the new land?

It's true that only the well-off could afford the fare. However, many colonists traveled as **indentured servants**. In return for a free ticket, they would work for their boss in the colonies for an agreed stretch of time (usually seven years).

JOURNEY TO JAMESTOWN

Let's take a look at the early pioneers who set the bar for the colonists who followed. It's a story of hunger, greed, and mysterious disappearances!

What was Jamestown?

It was the first *permanent* settlement, meaning it was the first settlement that survived. One of the earlier failed attempts happened in 1585, in what's now North Carolina. This settlement was called **Roanoke**, and it was founded by **Sir Walter Raleigh** and led by **John White**.

What happened to Roanoke?

The colonists' supplies were running low, so White went back to England to get help. However, war with Spain left him stuck in England for two years, and when he got back in 1590, everyone in Roanoke had vanished. To this day, no one knows what happened to the Roanoke colonists.

Why were the English so eager to try again, then?

Money talks! Eager for riches from the New World, **King James** I granted a charter to the Virginia Company in 1606, allowing them to found a colony to look for gold, silver, and other resources.

Hey... King James? Jamestown? Is that where the name came from?

Yes! The Virginia Company named their new settlement after King James himself

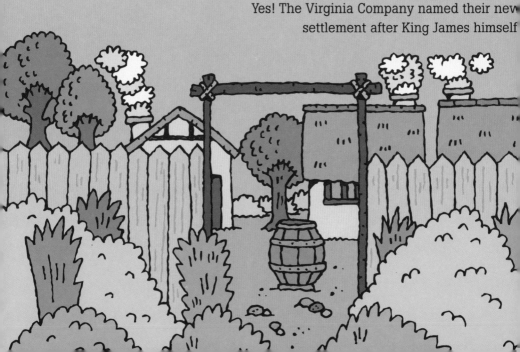

Were the Jamestown colonists successful?

Well, enough of them survived to keep the settlement going. Jamestown was built on marshland, a perfect place for disease. Tensions between the colonists and the local Native Americans (the *Algonquian*) grew quickly. Many colonists died from illness, starvation, or skirmishes, so by the summer of 1610, Jamestown's population had dwindled from over 500 to just 60.

Who was Powhatan?

It was the name of an Algonquian tribe as well as its chief. Powhatan tried to establish trade with Jamestown by meeting with their leader, John Smith, until Smith's frequent demands for corn put an end to their peace.

And John Smith?

John Smith was the president of Jamestown from 1608 to 1609, and he did a lot in that one year! Under his rule, if people wanted to eat, they had to work, which led to the rapid growth of the settlement.

What about Pocahontas?

Legends abound about Pocahontas, who was Chief Powhatan's daughter. Some stories suggest that she saved John Smith's life and willingly married John Rolfe, while others say that John Smith was never in danger, and that her marriage to John Rolfe came about after she was kidnapped. During the eight years of their marriage, the Jamestown settlers and Powhatan natives lived in peace.

Who was John Rolfe?

He turned Jamestown into a booming colony by learning how to grow tobacco. When he sent the first crop to England, his countrymen fell in love with it, and tobacco became the first cash crop in the New World.

11

A VICIOUS VOYAGE

Six hundred miles north of Jamestown, and 13 years after its founding, another group—called the Pilgrims—sailed for the New World aboard the *Mayflower*. This journey was anything but plain sailing for the passengers. Let's hear about the gruesome grub, storms, and sickness.

When did the Pilgrims set sail?
They waved goodbye to England on August 4, 1620, but trouble lay ahead. Their first ship, the *Speedwell*, sprang a leak and had to be abandoned in Plymouth, England. The 130 passengers and crew crowded onto the *Mayflower* and set sail in September. Not a great start!

Were all the passengers seeking religious freedom?
No. About a third of the passengers sought religious freedom. The rest of the 102 passengers were mainly tradesmen, who, for many reasons, were looking to start a new life.

the pilgrims' cows came to America on what ship?

the Mooooo-flower.

What was the *Mayflower's* destination?
The Pilgrims had been granted lands in Virginia, but storms threw the ship off course. After almost 3,000 miles (4,828 km) and 66 days at sea, the *Mayflower* arrived in Plymouth Bay on November 19, 1620.

Where did the passengers sleep?

The *Mayflower* was actually a merchant ship, and had been used for carrying a cargo of food, wood, and casks of wine. There were no cabins, windows, or individual beds for the passengers. They used curtains to create some privacy, and slept on wooden pallets, small landing boats, or hammocks.

What was the food like on board?

The ship stored food that was easy to preserve. Each passenger had a daily ration which could include salt beef, salted fish, beans, peas, porridge, and hardtack biscuits. Thirsty travelers drank beer or wine, as they were safer to slurp than water.

FACT OR
FICTION?

Did it get very smelly?

Yes! Time to hold your nose. With 130 travelers on board, it became one heck of a stinky ship! There was no water for washing clothes, and wooden buckets were used as toilets. In bad weather, the seasick passengers would be kept in their quarters below deck, with no fresh air and nowhere to empty their toilets.

Did everyone survive the storms, seasickness, and smelly conditions?

No. A servant, William Butten, died of illness, and a crew member was swept out to sea and drowned. Poor fellows!

THE FIRST INHABITANTS

The Europeans were not the first inhabitants of the New World. Their new neighbors had lived there for over 10,000 years.

Who lived in America before the Europeans?

The Native Americans! Different nations interacted with different settlements. The Puritans of New England met the Wampanoag, Jamestown met the Powhatan, early New Yorkers met the Leni Lenape, and James Oglethorpe of Savannah, Georgia, interacted with the Yamacraw.

How did the Native Americans feed themselves and their families?

The tribes were skilled in planting crops, hunting, and fishing. They cultivated corn, squash, and beans; caught herring and shellfish; and hunted deer, moose, and rabbit. Nuts, berries, greens, and mushrooms were gathered from forests, and bark, roots, leaves, and blossoms were used as medicine.

hat did the Native Americans live in?

ey constructed domed huts called **wetu** or **wigwam** (depending on the
ople), which were built near the coast. The Wampanoag lived in them
ring the growing season, and returned inland during winter. Frames were
ilt from saplings (young trees), and covered in dried cattails from swamps
marshes. Sounds cozy!

15

Did the Native Americans get along with the colonists?
Some did. For example, Chief Massasoit, the sachem (leader) of the Wampanoag, paid a visit to Plymouth to present gifts and sign a peace treaty that lasted for 50 years. On the other hand, Jamestown colonists demanded so many resources from the Powhatan that the Native Americans, who at first aided the colonists, soon turned hostile.

How did some of the colonists talk to the Native Americans?
Take Squanto for example. He was a Native American who had been kidnapped in 1614 by Europeans and was eventually returned to his New England homeland five years later. Squanto taught the Pilgrims to farm the new lands and acted as an interpreter during the peace negotiations.

hat was the worst thing the colonists brought to the New World?
sease. This was a disaster for the Native American tribes, whose bodies
d no protection against infections such as smallpox. Over 30,000 Native
nericans lived in Massachusetts in the 1620s, but by the end of the century,
) percent of them had been tragically killed by illness or warfare.

TOUGH TIMES AHEAD

Once they landed, the settlers faced an enormous task. They had no shelter, stored food, or knowledge of the new land and its inhabitants. Let's see if it was a disappointing disaster or a spectacular success!

Where did the settlers live when they first landed?
The Pilgrims lived aboard the *Mayflower* that first harsh winter.

What difficulties lay ahead?
The colonists suffered from illness, starvation, and freezing conditions. Diseases, including malaria and typhoid, swept through the new colony, and over half the original settlers died.

id the *Mayflower* stay in Plymouth?

o. In fact, the captain of the ship, Christopher Jones, offered to
ke any unhappy Pilgrims home on his way back, free of charge.

**punds like a good offer! How many Pilgrims
ecided to pack up and head back home?**

t a single one! The colonists had every faith that they would make a success
their new life. The *Mayflower* returned to England after the winter.

How do we know about the struggles that the first settlers endured?
Much of what we know about the first settlers is thanks to William Bradford. He wrote *Of Plymouth Plantation*, which is a record of the colony from 1620 to 1647.

Why didn't the settlers take turkeys to church?

they use FOWL language!

Did he do anything else?
To celebrate the settlers' first successful crop of corn, he organized a fantastic feast. This is known as the original Thanksgiving!

What did they serve at the first Thanksgiving?

A whole variety of tasty foods! For meats and seafood, they had goose, duck, venison (deer), fish, lobster, mussels, and, of course, turkey. The fruits and vegetables on the table were anything they could harvest, including beans, carrots, spinach, squash, raspberries, and grapes. Pumpkin and corn were there too, but they were served stewed and as porridge.

Who was invited to the first Thanksgiving?
The governor welcomed 91 of the Wampanoag to the celebration, including their sachem, Massasoit. Let's hope there were enough chairs!

21

AFRICAN-AMERICANS IN THE COLONIES

The story of African-Americans in Colonial America is a story of the struggle for freedom in the New World.

Were the Europeans the only ones to arrive in the colonies?
No. In the early 1600s some Africans came to America as sailors or indentured servants. In the decades that followed, however, farm owners and others turned from European indentured servants to enslaved Africans for their laborers. Throughout the colonial era, the colonies participated in an act called **slavery**, which meant people (known as **slaves**) were taken from their homes in Africa and forced to work in the New World. So many were brought to the colonies that by 1750, as much as 20 percent of the entire population consisted of current or former slaves.

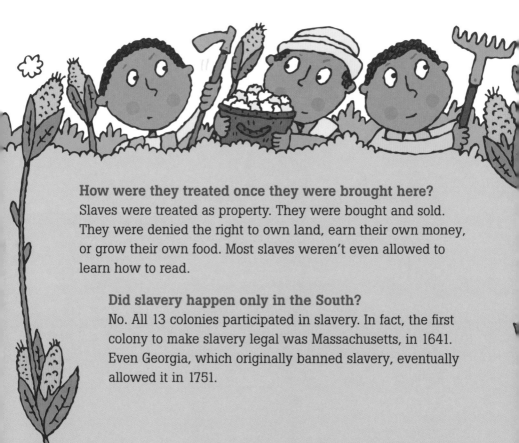

How were they treated once they were brought here?
Slaves were treated as property. They were bought and sold. They were denied the right to own land, earn their own money, or grow their own food. Most slaves weren't even allowed to learn how to read.

Did slavery happen only in the South?
No. All 13 colonies participated in slavery. In fact, the first colony to make slavery legal was Massachusetts, in 1641. Even Georgia, which originally banned slavery, eventually allowed it in 1751.

Did African-Americans have any hope for freedom in the colonies?

Indentured servants could work off their contracts. Slaves could sometimes purchase their own freedom, others were able to escape, and some were freed by their masters. In 1738, Fort Mose in Florida became the first free black settlement in Colonial America. It survived for decades, even repelling a British attack in 1740. Over time, many free African-Americans gravitated to cities, looking for jobs and school, church and community.

Who were some famous free men?

Crispus Attucks escaped slavery by working as a sailor. He became the first casualty in the struggle for American independence by leading a protest in 1770 against British soldiers, who opened fire in what became known as the Boston Massacre. Attucks is hailed as a Revolutionary patriot and hero.

Born free in Africa but captured as a boy, **Venture Smith** was sold into slavery in New England in 1739. After decades of hard labor, he managed to buy not only his freedom, but his wife and children's liberty too. Smith went on to own over 100 acres of land and three houses in Connecticut, and to write the earliest autobiography penned by a former slave.

The son of a free woman and a former slave, self-taught **Benjamin Banneker** became an accomplished inventor, astronomer, surveyor, mathematician, and writer. In 1752 he built one of the first clocks in the New World, and he later wrote and published *Banneker's Almanac*, which was filled with his own astronomical calculations and predictions.

FIRM FOUNDATIONS

The new settlers had to build new neighborhoods from the ground up—literally! Here's the lowdown on those early settlements.

What did the settlers' early lodgings look like?
The colonists worked hard to build shelters for themselves right away. The Jamestown settlers built simple thatched mud huts, and in Plymouth the Pilgrims built small wooden houses. Home sweet home!

How did the colonial settlements develop?
The first building to be constructed was usually a fort or meeting house. This was the central focus of every town, and it doubled as a place of worship. The settlements were defended with walls of tall sharpened logs and cannons perched on wooden platforms.

Did the Pilgrims build the first houses with bricks?
No! The houses in New England were built from wood, using the tools and nails brought over from England. The settlers assembled a wooden frame and used reeds and grasses to thatch the roof, leaving a hole for the chimney.

How long did it take to build these homes?

From start to finish, the process took two to three months, which was good news! The population boomed during the Great Migration of settlers from Europe, which began in 1629, lasted just over 10 years, and added almost 22,000 more settlers to the colony.

Were colonists allowed as much land as they wanted?

No. In Plymouth, all families were given plots of land 50 ft (15.24 m) deep. The width of the plot was 8 ft (2.44 m) for every family member.

How sturdy were these early homes?

Many early homes burnt to the ground when a stray spark landed on the thatched roof. Fed-up colonists banned thatched roofs in the mid-1600s, replacing dried reeds with slatted wood. Much more fire-resistant!

Do any colonial homes still exist?

Sure! Take a tour of Salem (Massachusetts), Portsmouth (New Hampshire), or Wethersfield (Connecticut) for a trip back in time. Don't forget your camera!

ON THE MENU

**What sorts of delicious dishes were on a colonist's table?
Let's take a peek at the plate!**

What would be served up to a hungry settler?
Colonists rose early and gulped down a cup of cider or
ale with a bowl of porridge or cornmeal pudding. Dinner
was served by the early afternoon and was the big meal
of the day. Supper would be a quick bedtime snack, with
either leftovers or plain old gruel.

How were the meals prepared?
The hard-working women of the household were responsible for preparing the
family meals. They had to light and look after the kitchen fire, carry the water,
dig up and pick the fruit and vegetables, and fetch the meat from the smoke-
house. Even the iron cooking pots took some lifting, and could weigh up to 40
pounds (18.14 kg). That's like picking up two and a half bowling balls!

d the Colonial Americans keep things cool in a refrigerator?

1 afraid not! Fruits and vegetables were preserved as jams, marmalades, :kles, and sauces. Sausages were made, and meat was smoked or salted. In nter, settlers in the northern colonies stored food outside, packed in snow. e houses to preserve fruits and vegetables would sometimes be built, and ice as sometimes shipped south in straw-packed crates.

ere the colonists picky eaters?

•, they couldn't afford to be picky eaters! They had to plant, grow, raise, and int whatever was available. Their daily provisions were beefed up with deer, bbits, and wild geese, and they caught fish, eel, lobster, and clams.

27

THE DAILY GRIND

The settlers weren't afraid to put in a hard day's work. Let's take a stroll through the settlement and get the lowdown on a colonist's nine-to-five!

What were some typical jobs in a colonial settlement?
The blacksmith was an essential tradesman, and would make and mend horseshoes, plowheads, tools, nails, and axes. A wheelwright was a skilled craftsman, working in wood and iron to assemble and repair carriage and wagon wheels.

A gunsmith had the know-how to make and repair guns, and so was skilled in both wood and metal work.

How did the colonies get their news?
Colonial newspapers would be put together by printers (who also printed books and legal documents). These newsletters would be written by the printers themselves, from pieces of newspaper from the Old World or other colonies, or from tips brought in by ordinary people.

Would a colonist be able to get a stylish new make-over?
From top to toe! As a colony grew, artisans could include a milliner (a hat maker), and a wigmaker. A tailor could stitch together a custom-made outfit, and the cobbler would create some sensible but stylish shoes.

Were these jobs held by men and women?

Not *these* jobs, no. In the 1600s, women were expected to marry by the age of 20, obey their husbands, raise a family, and work in the home. Without their hard work, a colony couldn't survive! Women cooked, mended, washed, and cultivated the vegetable garden. They made baskets, preserved food, tended the livestock, and were responsible for the children. They sold dairy goods and textiles to boost the family's income, and they managed the household budget.

What did Pilgrims use to bake cookies?

May-flour!

Were women allowed to go to school?

No, but most women were taught to read so that they could study the Bible. However, the Puritans felt that there was little need for them to learn to write.

Were there any roles for women outside the home?

Most communities would have a midwife to support expectant mothers through childbirth. Some settlements tried to attract experienced midwives with a wage and rent-free homes.

A DAY IN THE LIFE

The colonist's day-to-day life was very different from our own experiences today. Take a trip back in time to explore what they wore and much more!

Did all the settlers go to church?
They were in trouble if they didn't! If you were a no-show chances are you'd end up with a fine, or be put in the stocks (a long wooden board with holes for your feet, where you'd be placed for the town to see). Churchgoers sat on hard wooden benches, with sermons lasting up to two and a half hours.

What did the settlers do for fun?
Life wasn't just about church and chores! Although they didn't celebrate Christmas, the colonists made merry at festivals and weddings, enjoying a cup of wine or beer and dancing the night away (as long as the men and women didn't touch).

What was an average day like for a colonial kid?
From an early age, children in the settlements worked in the fields, fetched water, babysat, prepared food, and tended the livestock. Children were educated at home, with lessons concentrating on obedience, Bible studies, reading, spelling, and arithmetic.

So, was it all work and no play?
With their parents' permission, kids were allowed a little time off each day. Children ran races to exercise their bodies and played checkers to give their minds a workout. They played with dolls, blew bubbles, and enjoyed word games and tongue twisters.

What is a tongue twister a colonial kid might have liked?
Try this out! "Don drunk drink in a dish; where's the dish Don drunk drink in?"

Did the Puritans only wear black clothes?
No, they didn't! They wore their best clothes to have their portraits painted, and their finest gear was black. A colonist's day-to-day wear was made of wool and linen in brown, brick-red, yellow, green, and blue. Fancy!

hat were the fashions of the day?
:n wore loose linen shirts, knee-length breeches, long woollen socks, and ain leather shoes, as well as tricorne (three-cornered), wide-brimmed, or itted hats. Women dressed in a loose shift, a petticoat, a long gown, and an ron. Woolly socks, simple leather shoes, and a puffy cap completed the outfit.

hat about the colonial kids?
)m the age of six or seven, children wore mini-versions of their parents' thes. Babies wore long sleeved gowns, and as they learned to walk, **leading aps** would be added, to help keep the baby upright and balanced. Toddlers re padded headgear called a **pudding cap**, designed to protect the child's ad if they wobbled over.

COLONIAL CRIMES AND PURITAN PUNISHMENT

What penalties were handed out to colonists who stepped out of line? Were they strict and severe, or fair and just?

What sort of punishments were there for bad behavior?

The law was tough and the sentences were harsh. After three years at sea, Bostonian Captain Kemble made the mistake of kissing his wife on a Sunday. That earned him several hours in the stocks!

Branding was common practice, when a letter would be burnt onto the offender's skin as a sign of their crime. Forgery was an F, and R was for rogue. If you committed a burglary, a B would be burnt onto your hand.

Can it get any worse?

The pillory stood in the settlement's main square, and was a wooden upright board with holes for the culprit's head and hands. In 1648, John Goneere was convicted of lying in a Maryland court, and was nailed to the pillory by both ears and whipped for good measure.

**hat sorts of school punishments and tortuous treatments
ere there for kids in colonial times?**

hips, canes, paddles, and birch rods could all be found in a teacher's
esk drawer. Badly behaved children were tapped on the head with a
heavy thimble, or forced to try and balance on a one-legged stool.

Were children given reward stickers or classroom treats?

What do you think? A schoolmaster's common
punishment would be to force an offending child to
wear signs with proclamations such as "Tell-Tale,"
"Bite-finger Baby," and "Idle-Boy."

FACT OR
FICTION?

e these punishments kept to the schoolroom?

I afraid not. The colonists employed a **tithingman** in church who carried a
lg pole with a wooden knob on one end, and a feather on the other. If he
sotted people snoozing during the sermon, he would tap children on the head
wth the knob end, and tickle the older people with the feather.

HOLD THE FRONT PAGE!

The crops were growing, settlements were expanding and trade was thriving. Was life calm in the colonies? No! Let's take a look at the headlines.

NEW NETHERLAND SURRENDERS!
NEWS JUST IN!

After fighting three naval wars, the English seized control of the New Netherland colony in 1664. King Charles II handed it to his brother, James, Duke of York, who re-named it New York.

Did the English send the Dutch packing?
Not at all! They were allowed to stay put, keep their pubs open, and practice their religion in freedom.

Why did King Charles II go to the dentist?

To get his teeth crowned!

WAR IS DECLARED!
NATIVE AMERICANS REACH BREAKING POINT!

King Philip's War (1675-1676) was a last-ditch attempt by the Native Americans to get rid of the English settlers. The war came to an end when King Philip was captured and assassinated, one of 3,000 Native Americans that had been killed in the conflict.

Why was the Native American leader called King Philip?
That was the title given to him by the English.
His native name was Metacomet.

EXCLUSIVE! WILLIAM PENN FOUNDS NEW COLONY!

enn had a vision of a colony that was a safe haven for Quakers, like himself, nd for other persecuted religious groups. In 1681, he explained his plan to ing Charles II, who agreed and granted Penn a tract of land.

What did he name it?
Pennsylvania, which combined his family name of "Penn" and the Latin word for forest land, "Sylvania."

READ ALL ABOUT IT!
GEORGIA! THE COLONY WITH A DIFFERENCE!

Vealthy Englishman James Oglethorpe had a vision! He wanted to create a olony using the talents of convicted debtors and the unemployed. King George greed to a charter in 1732, and Oglethorpe got to work on his list of rules and egulations.

/hat were Oglethorpe's main ideas?
Georgia, land ownership would be limited to 50 acres
er person, and slavery, Catholics, lawyers, and liquor would
e banned.

PEACE!
THE FRENCH AND INDIAN WAR IS OVER!

1e French had expanded their territory into the Ohio River Valley, and had ntered into a number of conflicts and skirmishes with British colonists. The itish finally declared war in 1756. Seven years of violent conflict ensued, but en, in 1763, it came to an end at a peace conference.

What was the result?
The British Prime Minister William Pitt saw the victory as a way to expand the British empire. He borrowed huge sums of money to pay for the war and was rewarded with the French surrender of Canada.

THE ROAD TO WAR

As the colonies grew and prospered, the colonists became downbeat about being ruled by the English thousands of miles away. Let's look at some factors that led to the Revolutionary War.

What are taxes?

A tax is an amount of money that workers and businesses pay to their government in return for services such as schools, roads, the police force and libraries.

If the colonies were prospering, why did the colonists begin to feel fed-up?

Relations with the Brits were becoming strained. Although each colony governed itself, the British king was still in overall control. Laws and taxes were forced on them by a government thousands of miles away, and they got little in return. The British government, deep in debt, insisted on raising taxes

HEAR YE! HEAR YE!

Did the colonists "put up, or shut up"?
The colonists felt that if they were forced to pay tax to the British government, then in return they should have a seat and a vote in Parliament. They came up with the anti-British slogan "No taxation without representation." The fight back had begun!

What sorts of taxes and acts did the British government inflict on the colonies?
While the colonists faced several new taxes and laws, here are some of the most important:

Navigation Acts • 1660 Restricted trade to English ships and taxed tobacco, sugar, and other items not available in England

Molasses Act • 1733 A heavy tax on sugar, molasses and wine

Currency Act • 1764 Limited the use of currency created by New England colonies

Quartering Act • 1765 This forced colonists to pay for food, drink, and accommodation for the British troops

Stamp Act • 1765 A tax on newspapers, leaflets, legal papers, and playing cards

Townsend Act • 1767 Duties placed on many imported items including glass, lead, paint, paper, and tea

Tea Act • 1773 This allowed low-cost tea to be sold direct to the colonies, undermining the New England Tea Merchants

What else upset the colonists?
King George III issued the Proclamation of 1763, which declared that all lands west of the colonies were off-limits! Only the British government could negotiate with Native Americans, and merchants would need a license to travel or trade.

REBEL! REBEL!

Life in the colonies was proving to be extremely taxing, and the English had pushed the colonists to their breaking point. Enough was enough!

How did the colonist rebels organize themselves?
They put together the Sons of Liberty. This was a secret club of patriots who targeted the hated tax collectors. Many of these collectors were driven out of the town, and the ones that didn't run fast enough were covered in tar and feathers!

Did women form a Daughters of Liberty society?
Yes, and they were very effective! They refused to buy British goods and boycotted British tea. They organized huge spinning bees, where they would weave cloth to reduce the need for British textiles.

NOTABLE DAUGHTERS OF LIBERTY

Betsy Ross
Sewed the first American flag

Esther DeBerdt Reed
Raised $300,000 for the American troops

Mercy Otis Warren
Wrote pamphlets and plays about life under British rule

Catherine Moore Barry
Warned the colonist troops of any approaching enemy soldiers

What was the Boston Massacre of 1770?
It started with a disagreement between a bunch of colonists and a British soldier. Tension increased, and before long, sticks and blocks of ice were being thrown at the soldier. British reinforcements arrived and, in the scuffle, a shot was fired into the crowd. Other soldiers followed suit, and the Boston Massacre resulted in the unfortunate deaths of five colonists.

What was the Boston Tea Party?
On December 16, 1773, the Sons of Liberty, led by Samuel Adams, wanted to let the British government know exactly what they thought about the unwelcome Tea Act. They headed to the harbor and, dressed as Native Americans, clambered on board the British ship, *Dartmouth*. The rebels dumped 342 chests of British tea overboard, an event now remembered as the Boston Tea Party.

What was the American colonists' favorite tea?

Liberty!

Did this teach the greedy Brits a lesson?
Nope! They closed the harbor, ended self-rule in the colonies, and took away some colonies' lands by extending the Canadian border. These laws were called the Intolerable Acts.

What was the colonies' response to the Intolerable Acts?
Twelve of the colonies met in secret to form the first Continental Congress, in September 1774. Georgia sat this one out.

What did the first Continental Congress decide to do?
They challenged the British government's right to tax them. They agreed to boycott all British goods in December of that year. If the acts were still in place by September 1775, then export trade with Britain would end too.

THE MIDNIGHT RIDE

British troops had revenge on their mind, and the patriots needed a heads-up. The Sons of Liberty kept a close eye on the British "Redcoat" soldiers in Boston to try to learn of their plans. Along with them, there were several other heroes who helped raise the alarm.

What were the British troops planning to do?
The patriots had heard that the British were preparing an advance and that they had targeted revolutionary leaders John Hancock and Samuel Adams. Riders were sent to warn them, and on April 18, 1775, Paul Revere and William Dawes galloped to Lexington, taking two different routes.

One if by land, two if by se

Did Revere and Dawes have a back-up warning system?
Yes! Revere had arranged that sexton Robert Newman would light lanterns in the North Church steeple to communicate with colonists in Charleston. If the British were advancing by land, then one lantern would be lit. Two lights meant that they were coming by sea.

Was the ride a success? Did the message make it through?
Paul Revere arrived in Lexington first, and warned of the Redcoats' advance along the Charles River. Dawes and Revere headed out to Concord, but never made it there. On the journey, they had met fellow rider, Samuel Prescott. With his skilled horsemanship and knowledge of local routes, Prescott finally delivered Revere's warning to colonial troops from Concord. Hooray!

What an eventful night! Was it time for bed?

Nowhere near! Warned that the Redcoats were coming, a group of colonial troops, called **minutemen** (because they could be ready to fight very quickly), began to assemble in Lexington and Concord—Lexington to protect Hancock and Adams, and Concord because the colonists' stash of weapons was there. When the British showed up in Lexington, men from both sides stood facing each other, but then chaos reigned. A gun was fired, named **the shot heard round the world**, and the Revolutionary War had begun!

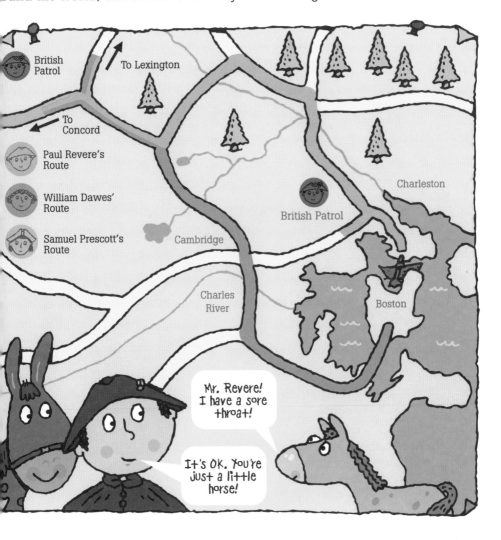

I DO DECLARE!

Independence from Britain was announced in 1776, but there were many hurdles to overcome. Many famous fellows worked together to achieve self-rule.

Who was the leader of the colonial army?
Less than a month after the Midnight Ride, the Continental Congress met for the second time. Led by John Hancock, they chose George Washington to be the man who would lead their troops. Good decision!

Were the colonists determined to go to war?
Far from it! A year before the Declaration of Independence was signed, the congress had sent King George III the Olive Branch Petition, which would give the colonists rights while keeping their loyalty to the Crown. Grumpy George refused to read it, and in a speech to Parliament, he declared he would "put a speedy end to these disorders." Well, at least they tried!

What is the Declaration of Independence?
It's America's most important document. It let the world know that the 13 colonies were no longer a part of the British Empire. They had founded a brand-new nation: the United States of America! Hooray!

Who wrote the Declaration of Independence?
Five delegates were chosen to draft the document: Benjamin Franklin, John Adams, Roger Sherman, Robert Livingston, and of course, Thomas Jefferson. However, Jefferson wrote the document, as he had such great handwriting.

Who signed it?
56 men went to the Pennsylvania state house (now known as Independence Hall) in Philadelphia to sign the Declaration of Independence. Of those signatures, John Hancock's is the largest. He said that he wanted King George III to be able to read it without his glasses.

What is the Liberty Bell?
At the Declaration's first public reading, citizens were summoned to Independence Hall by the ringing of its bell, which is now known as the Liberty Bell. Nowadays, the bell is rung 13 times (one for each colony) every 4th of July.

FACT OR FICTION?

Is there really a smudge on the Declaration of Independence?
Indeed! Thomas Jefferson made a slip-up when he wrote "subjects" instead of "citizens."

* Citizens *

~~jects~~

I don't think anyone will notice!

The next job was to design an official seal for the new nation. Which design was selected?
The Bald Eagle! Not everyone was happy though. Ben Franklin described the bald eagle as "a bird of bad moral character." You can't please everyone!

How rude!

THIS MEANS WAR!

The struggle for independence came at a price. It's a tale of bloody battles, terrible traitors, dire defeats, and terrific triumphs!

Was the Continental Army a first-rate fighting force?
Hardly! Washington was a reluctant commander-in-chief, and had little experience in leading a large military operation. The army was a shabby crew of colonists who were poorly trained, ill-equipped, and half-starved.

What was the first thing Washington did to turn this army into a force that could stand up to an empire?
He organized the ragtag rabble that had been controlled by each individual colony into a force of 80,000 soldiers in three divisions, six brigades, and thirty-six regiments. However, no uniform was provided, pay was poor, and rifles were often homemade.

id the colonies join forces with other nations to help
efeat the British?
ien sûr! (That's French for "of course"!) The patriots formed an alliance with
rance, and received supplies, arms, ammunition, and uniforms, as well as
oops and naval support. *Merci!*

What was the colonists' first win?
he capture of Fort Ticonderoga was the first "official" victory for the patriots,
May 1775. Amazingly, no one was killed, and the Continental Army gained
ver 50 cannons. It took 56 days for the 60 tons of artillery to be dragged 300
iles by ox-drawn sleds to Boston.

Did the patriots have an easy ride?
Not at all, but they did give the Brits a run for their money! At the Battle of
Bunker Hill, in June 1775, the Americans proved to be an effective opposition.
They'd had advanced warning of the British plans, so they set up their
defenses on Bunker Hill and Breed's Hill overnight.

The British attacked, and the Americans fought bravely, despite their
ammunition running low. The British eventually won, but had lost
226 men in battle.

**British troops forced the patriots to evacuate
New York and Boston. How did Washington
get even?**
On Christmas night 1776, George Washington and
2,400 of his men crossed the icy Delaware River
in one of the conflict's biggest gambles. The British
had hired around 30,000 German Hessian troops,
some of whom were camped in Trenton, on the
opposite side of the river. Having celebrated the
holidays in style, the Hessian soldiers were
taken aback by the patriots' attack. In just
45 minutes, Washington's troops seized over
900 prisoners, and the hungry American soldiers
captured much-needed food, supplies, and
ammunition. Happy holidays!

ere there any traitors?

:nedict Arnold was a brave patriot fighter in the early years of the war.
₂ played important roles at the capture of Fort Ticonderoga, and in following
ıttles was shot in the leg and crippled when his horse fell on the same limb.

₂ became furious as Congress passed him by for promotion and, in revenge,
rned traitor. He handed over the fort he commanded in the Hudson River to
e enemy, in exchange for a considerable amount of cash and a high-ranking
ıst in the British Army. Let's call him the Revolutionary War's "hero to zero."

hich battle brought the brutal conflict to an end?

1780, the French joined the Americans in a determined effort to defeat the
itish. A year later, they laid siege to Yorktown, Virginia, and bombarded the
ıemy for 22 days. The Redcoats' General Lord Charles Cornwallis eventually
ırrendered. Victory to America!

INDEPENDENCE!

After several long and punishing years, the Revolutionary War finally came to an end in 1783. The colonies were now a brand-new country. Hooray! Was it a time for celebration, or concern for the future?

What happened when the war ended?
The British and the colonists met and came up with a document called the Treaty of Paris. In this treaty, the British recognized the United States of America as its own country and withdrew all their troops. The borders were set, America had to pay off any debt, and its new citizens promised not to bully any of the king's supporters. All lands east of the Mississippi were returned to the Americans, and the West could now be settled.

Did the United States want a king or queen of their own?
No! They chose to have a democratic government, with leaders elected by the people. George Washington became the first President of the United States of America in 1789.

How did America's leaders decide on their new nation's laws and regulations?
Five men, called the framers, were chosen to write the Constitution of the United States. This would give the government the powers to:

- ★ collect taxes
- ★ control trade
- ★ make arrangements with foreign countries
- ★ declare war and form an army and navy
- ★ issue coin money
- ★ make laws

After a bit of debating and negotiating, the 13 states signed the Constitution in May 1790.

What is red, white, blue, and yellow?

A star-spangled banana!

CHECK OUT ALL OF THE FANTASTIC FACTS IN THIS SENSATIONAL SERIES!

100 Questions about Bugs

100 Questions about Colonial America

100 Questions about Outer Space

100 Questions about Pirates